ACTIVE
LEARNING

in
SCIENCE

W9-CEJ-195

GLOBE FEARON EDUCATIONAL PUBLISHER
A Division of Simon & Schuster
Upper Saddle River, New Jersey

Project Editors: Lynn W. Kloss, Ann Clarkson, Bernice Golden
Editorial and Marketing Manager: Diane Galen
Executive Editor: Joan Carrafiello
Writer: Sandra Widener
Editorial Supervisor: Linda Zierdt-Warshaw
Production Manager: Kurt Scherwatzky
Production Editor: Alan Dalgleish
Marketing Managers: Margaret Rakus, Donna Frasco
Interior Electronic Design: Elaine Kilcullen
Electronic Page Production: Elaine Kilcullen
Cover Design: Mimi Raihl
Artists: Michael Adams, Ted Enik, Mapping Specialists Limited,
  Nina Wallace

Reviewer:
Dorie L. Knaub, B.A., M.S.
  Special Education Specialist
  Downey Unified School District
  Downey, CA

Printed in the United States of America.   2 3 4 5 6 7 8 9 10 99 98

ISBN: 0-8359-3364-4

GLOBE FEARON EDUCATIONAL PUBLISHER
A Division of Simon & Schuster
Upper Saddle River, New Jersey

Contents

Activity

The Meaning of Green

What do plants need to live? Do they need sunlight? Do an experiment to find the answer. Then summarize what you find.

MAKE A PLAN

Here is what you will need.

_____ 3 small plants of the same size

_____ a box to cover one plant   _____ a cup

_____ water   _____ a metric ruler

Review the activity. Estimate how long it will take.

_____

I will work

_____ by myself   _____ with a partner   _____ in a group

Did You Know . . .

A farmer grew the tallest tomato plant in the world. It was 16 meters (53 feet) high. That is taller than a five-story building.

53 feet (16 meters)

40 feet (12 meters)

30 feet (9 meters)

20 feet (6 meters)

10 feet (3 meters)

0 feet (0 meters)

Could that farmer have grown that plant without sunlight? Write your **hypothesis,** or guess, here. _____

Doing Research

Plants do not have to eat. They make food in their leaves. This process is called **photosynthesis** (foht-oh-SIN-thuh-sis).

How does this work? Look at the picture.

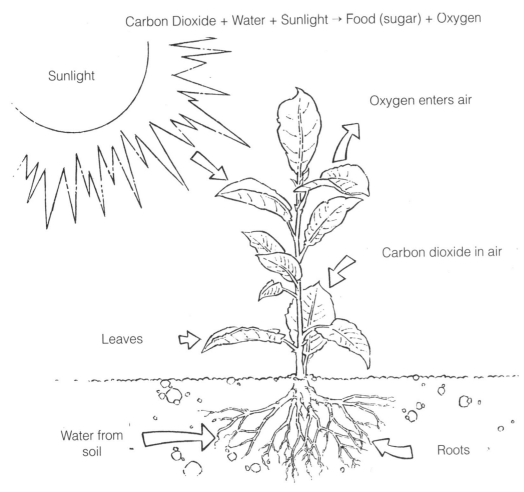

Carbon Dioxide + Water + Sunlight → Food (sugar) + Oxygen

Sunlight

Oxygen enters air

Carbon dioxide in air

Leaves

Water from soil

Roots

- The plant's leaves take in sunlight.
- The leaves also take in a gas from the air. That gas is called carbon dioxide.
- The plant takes in water from the soil.
- Sunlight combines the water and carbon dioxide. That makes sugar.
- The sugar feeds the plant.

How important is sunlight in this process?
Do the experiment on the next page to find the answer.

Collecting Information

Start with three plants of about the same height.
Label the plants: Plant 1, Plant 2, and Plant 3.
Use the ruler to measure each plant.
How many millimeters tall is each plant?
Write the answers here.

Plant 1 _____ Plant 2 _____ Plant 3 _____

Find a sunny place. Put Plant 1 there.
Find a shady place. Put Plant 2 there.
Cover Plant 3 with the box. Make sure that no light can get in.

What do you think will happen to each plant?

Write your **hypothesis** here. _____

_____

_____

For the next two weeks, give only water to your plants. Give each plant the same amount. Do not water the plants too much. Every other day, look at each plant.

Fill in this chart for the next two weeks. Measure each plant in millimeters.

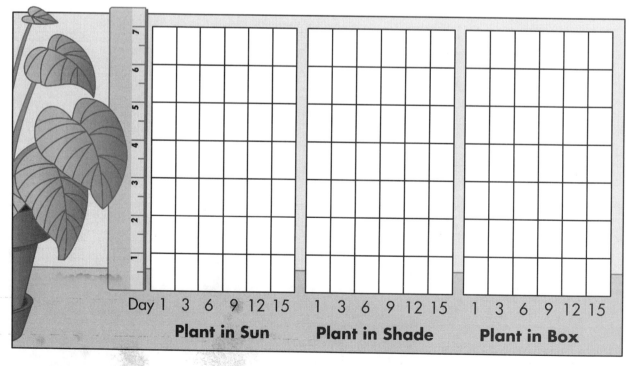

Analyzing Information

Write your answers to these questions below.

1. What were you trying to find out?

2. What was your hypothesis?

3. What happened?

4. Was your hypothesis correct?

Showing What You Know

On another piece of paper, draw pictures of the plants after the experiment. Write under each one why the plant looks the way it does.

Activity 2

For the Birds

Like all living things, birds need food. Can you plan to attract different birds with different foods? Find out in this activity. Then make a poster for bird lovers.

MAKE A PLAN

Here is what you will need.

_____ 4 bird feeders or trays   _____ a bird book

_____ sunflower seeds   _____ mixed birdseed

_____ binoculars (if you have them)   _____ poster board and markers or paints

_____ peanuts in the shell   _____ notebook

_____ raisins

Review the activity. Estimate how long it will take.

_____

I will work

_____ by myself   _____ with a partner   _____ in a group

Did You Know . . .

There are more than 9,700 kinds of birds. The smallest is the bee hummingbird. It is about 5 centimeters (2 inches) long. The largest bird is the ostrich. It can grow to 2.7 meters (9 feet) long.

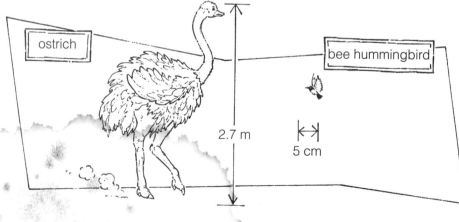

ostrich

bee hummingbird

2.7 m

5 cm

Doing Research

Why do different kinds of birds look and act differently?
They have different **adaptations**. An adaptation helps a
living thing survive in its environment. Feathers are an
adaptation all birds have. Feathers help keep birds warm.
They also help most birds fly.

- Each kind of bird is adapted to its life. Ducks have
  webbed feet. These feet help ducks swim in water.

- Hawks have long, sharp claws. They use these claws to
  catch animals. Hawks eat these animals for food.

- Birds use their beaks to get food. The shape of a bird's beak
  is an adaptation for getting food. Look at these birds and
  their beaks. See if you can tell what food each bird eats.

Collecting Information

You will find out what kinds of foods birds eat. You will also find out if certain kinds of birds eat certain kinds of foods.

To do this, follow these steps.

1. Put a different kind of food in each bird feeder or tray. Use the same amount of each kind of bird feed.

2. Put each feeder or tray in a place that you can see. It should be a place that birds sometimes visit.

3. Visit each bird feeder each day for 2 weeks. Observe each feeder for 5–10 minutes. Each time you visit, bring your notebook. At the top of the paper, write the day and the time. On the paper, note these things.

☑ The kinds of birds that you see at each feeder.

☑ How many birds are at each feeder.

4. Draw a sketch of each bird that you see.

5. Write what feed the bird is eating. Then note these things about the bird:

☑ What shape is its body?

☑ What shape are its feet? Does it have long or short toes? Does it have long or short claws?

☑ What color or colors is it?

☑ What shape is its beak?

Answering these questions will help you **identify**, or find the names of, the birds that you see.

Your note for each bird will look something like the drawing on this page.

When you come back to the class, look at the bird book. Try to identify each bird that you saw at the feeders. Write the name of each bird you think that you saw next to your notes about that bird.

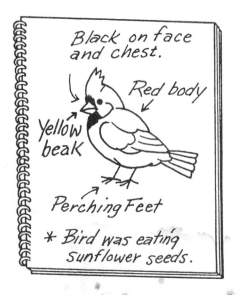

Black on face and chest.

Red body

Yellow beak

Perching Feet

* Bird was eating sunflower seeds.

Analyzing Information

Use the information that you gathered to make a poster for bird lovers.

Your poster should have this information.

☑ What kinds of birds you saw.

☑ What they ate. Look at the bird food left in each feeder. What food did the birds like most? Put that information on the poster.

Your poster should have a headline that tells people what the poster is about. Make a design that makes people want to look at the poster. Make the poster easy to understand. Here are some poster ideas.

Showing What You Know

Present your poster to the class. Explain:

☑ Your headline and why you chose it.

☑ What kinds of birds you saw.

☑ How you identified them.

☑ What kind of food the birds ate most often.

Activity 3

How's Your Nutrition?

You need food to stay alive. Some foods are better for you than others. How well do you eat? Keep track for one day. Then make a plan to eat better.

WORDS YOU NEED

vitamin—chemicals the body needs to do its work

nutrition—eating and using food

MAKE A PLAN

Here is what you will need.

_____ a pencil   _____ a clipboard

Review the activity. Estimate how long it will take.

_____

I will work

_____ by myself   _____ with a partner   _____ in a group

Did You Know . . .

During the 1800s, many people in Asia began to get a disease. It was called *beriberi*. A doctor found that beriberi came from eating white rice. Up to then, everyone ate brown rice. Brown rice still had **vitamins** in it. When the rice was polished, it turned white and lost its vitamins. People needed the vitamins in brown rice to keep from getting beriberi. People ate brown rice again and got well. What you eat does matter.

Doing Research

Look at the chart below. It shows how much of each kind of food you should eat each day. If you follow the chart, you will have the **nutrition** that you need to stay healthy.

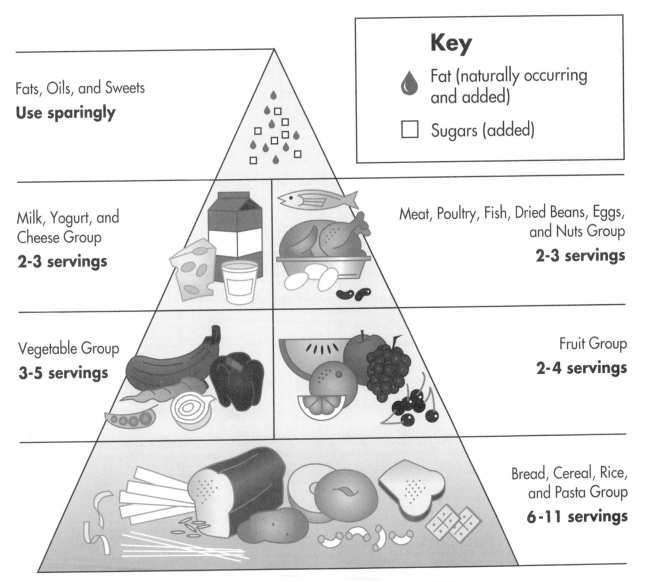

Key

💧 Fat (naturally occurring and added)

☐ Sugars (added)

Fats, Oils, and Sweets
Use sparingly

Milk, Yogurt, and Cheese Group
2-3 servings

Meat, Poultry, Fish, Dried Beans, Eggs, and Nuts Group
2-3 servings

Vegetable Group
3-5 servings

Fruit Group
2-4 servings

Bread, Cereal, Rice, and Pasta Group
6-11 servings

The chart talks about servings.
What is a serving?

- For meat, it is a piece the size of the palm of your hand.
- A half cup of most fruits and vegetables is a serving.
- A half cup of milk is a serving.
- A slice of bread is a serving.

Collecting Information

Pay attention to the foods that you eat for 1 day. Each time you eat, list all the foods in the chart below. List the drinks you had. Estimate how many servings you had of each kind of food or drink.

	What I ate for	Number of servings
Breakfast		
Lunch		
Dinner		

At the end of the day, write what you ate in the triangle chart below. Tell how many servings you had of each kind of food.

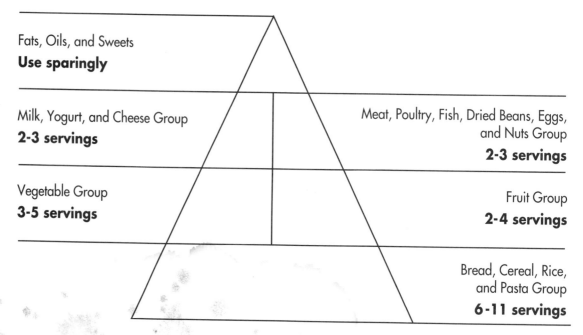

Fats, Oils, and Sweets
Use sparingly

Milk, Yogurt, and Cheese Group
2-3 servings

Meat, Poultry, Fish, Dried Beans, Eggs, and Nuts Group
2-3 servings

Vegetable Group
3-5 servings

Fruit Group
2-4 servings

Bread, Cereal, Rice, and Pasta Group
6-11 servings

Analyzing Information

Take a look at your triangle chart. Use it to help you with this report.

1. Circle the number of servings of bread that you ate.

0–5   6–11   12 or more

2. Circle the number of servings of fruit that you ate.

0–1   2–4   5 or more

3. Circle the number of servings of vegetables that you ate.

0–2   3–5   6 or more

4. Circle the number of servings of meat and fish that you ate.

0–1   2–3   4 or more

5. Circle the number of servings of milk, yogurt, and cheese that you ate.

0–1   2–3   4 or more

6. Look at the chart on page 11. Compare it to what you ate. What should you do to eat better? _____

_____

_____

_____

Showing What You Know

Take your report home. Talk with the people in your family. Help them plan a healthy menu for tomorrow. Write the menu you plan on a separate sheet of paper.

Activity 4

Get Moving!

Exercise keeps your body strong. How much exercise do you get each week? Keep track of what you do. Then write a plan for how to keep yourself fit.

MAKE A PLAN

Here is what you will need.

_____ pencil

Review the activity. Estimate how long it will take.

_____

I will work

_____ by myself _____ with a partner _____ in a group

WORDS YOU NEED

exercise—moving your body to become physically fit

muscles—organs of the body that allow movement

Did You Know . . .

There are dozens of ways to get **exercise**. Here are some ways Americans exercise. Which activity do you think is the most popular? Which is the least popular? Number the activities in order.

____ playing ice hockey   ____ bicycling

____ walking   ____ snow skiing

____ running   ____ ice skating

____ hiking   ____ playing tennis

____ swimming   ____ playing football

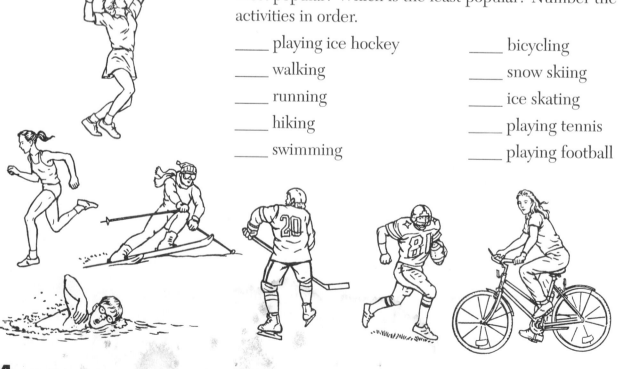

Doing Research

Why is it so important to get moving?
Here's why.
When you exercise, this is what happens.

- Your heart beats more often.

- You breathe more often.

- Your body uses more energy.

Why is this good for you?

- Your heart becomes stronger. It works better.

- Your **muscles** become stronger. They can work longer.

- Your whole body becomes more fit. You can work longer and not grow tired.

You can find out how exercise changes your heart rate and breathing rate.

1. Sit at your desk quietly. Count the number of times you breathe in and out in 1 minute. Write the number here.

_____

2. Place your hand on your chest. Count the number of times your heart beats in 1 minute. Write the number here.

_____

3. Run in place for 1 minute.

4. Now count the number of times you breathe in 1 minute. Write the number here. _____

5. Count how many times your heart beats in 1 minute. Write the number here. _____

How did this exercise change your heart rate? _____

_____

How did this exercise change your breathing rate? _____

_____

Collecting Information

Keep track of the exercise you do for one week.
Here are some things that count as exercise:

running   ice skating
walking   playing hockey
biking   playing soccer
raking leaves   playing football
sweeping   skiing

All sports count as exercise. Anything else you do that
makes you move around counts, too.

Keep an exercise diary. Write what you did every day.
Write how long you did it.

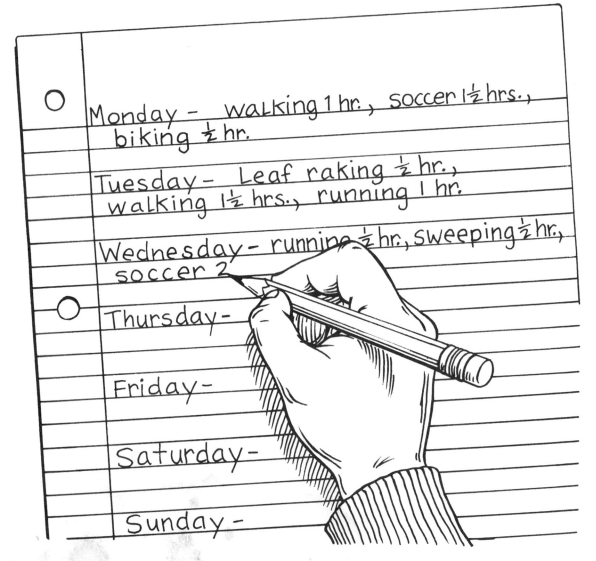

Monday – walking 1 hr., soccer 1½ hrs., biking ½ hr.

Tuesday – Leaf raking ½ hr., walking 1½ hrs., running 1 hr.

Wednesday – running ½ hr., sweeping ½ hr., soccer 2

Thursday –

Friday –

Saturday –

Sunday –

Analyzing Information

You should get 30 minutes of exercise at least three times a week. More is better.

Look at what you did during the last week.
Add up the minutes that you exercised. How much did you exercise? _____

Did you get enough exercise this week to stay healthy?
Circle yes or no on the diagram below. Then follow the arrows from the word you circled, and answer the questions.

Yes ▼	**No** ▼
Write what you like to do. _____ _____	What do you do now? _____ _____
What would you like to try? _____ _____	What else could you do? _____ _____
When can you try this? _____ _____ _____	What would you like to try? _____ _____
	When can you try this? _____

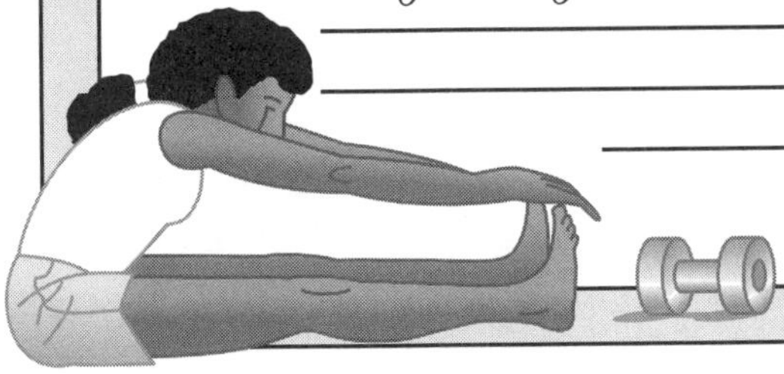

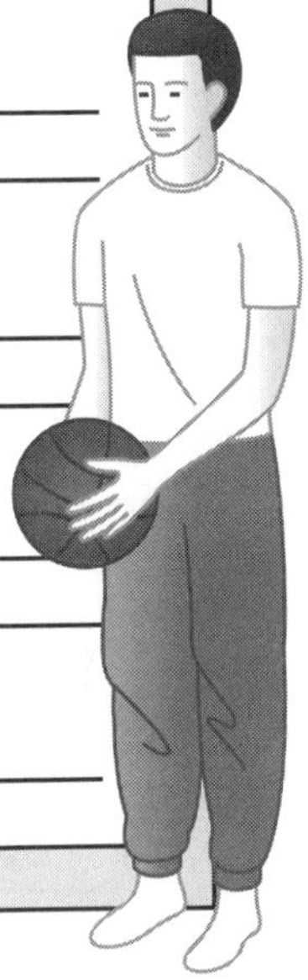

Showing What You Know

Write a plan for how you will get more exercise. If you get enough, write how you can improve what you do. You could try something new. You could try different things to stay fit. Use the blank space below to write your plan.

I _____ get enough exercise. I get about _____ minutes of exercise each week. The things I do to get exercise are _____ .
To get more exercise I would like to try _____ .
I could also _____ .

Activity 5

The Mystery of Fingerprints

Your fingerprints are different from everyone else's. Because of this, police can solve crimes using fingerprints. Find out how they do it. Then solve a fingerprint mystery.

WORDS YOU NEED

skin—largest organ of the body

dermis—inner layer of the skin

epidermis—outer layer of the skin

pores—tiny openings in the skin

MAKE A PLAN

Here is what you will need.

_____ white poster board

_____ heavy white paper cut into 2-inch by 2-inch pieces

_____ black ink pad

_____ paper towels

_____ hand soap

Review the activity. Estimate how long it will take.

_____

I will work

_____ by myself _____ with a partner _____ in a group

Did You Know . . .

The ancient Chinese were the first to use fingerprints to identify people. They saw that fingerprints were different. When people signed important papers, they put their fingerprints on them. That made the papers legal.

Doing Research

Skin is an organ. It is the largest organ of the body. There are some things about skin that are the same in everyone.

- Everyone has a **dermis**. This is the inner layer of skin. It is alive.

- Everyone has an **epidermis** (ep-uh-DER-muhs). This is the part of the skin that you see. It is made up of dead cells.

- Everyone has **pores** in his or her skin. Pores are tiny openings in the skin. One thing pores do is let sweat leave the body. Sweat helps to cool the body when the body becomes too hot.

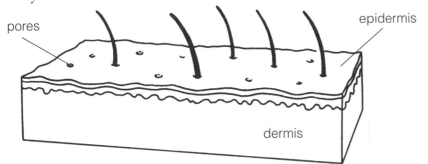

All people have differences in their skin, too. Look at the tips of your fingers. Can you see tiny lines? The lines form a pattern. That is your fingerprint. There are names for general patterns in fingerprints. But no two people have exactly the same pattern. Only you have the pattern on your finger.

People who fight crime use fingerprints to identify a person. Imagine that a robber leaves fingerprints on a window. Later, the police find the fingerprints. They fingerprint the person they think is the robber. If the prints match, the police have their robber.

Collecting Information

What do your fingerprints look like?
Here's how to find out.

1. Wash your hands. Dry them on a paper towel.

2. Open the ink pad. It should be the kind of ink pad that people use for rubber stamps.

3. Roll the thumb on your right hand from left to right on the ink pad. Now carefully pick up your thumb. Roll it from left to right in the space on the chart marked "Right Hand, Thumb." Wash your inked finger.

4. Repeat step 3 for each finger and for your other thumb. Wash the inked finger after each print.

5. Let the ink in the chart dry.

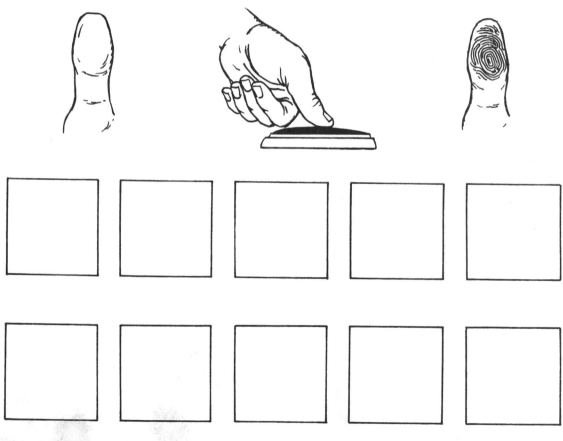

Analyzing Information

Now you will try to solve a mystery. Work in groups of four people.

1. Have a small piece of paper for each person. Number one side of each piece from 1 to 4. Have each person remember the number on his or her piece of paper.

2. Have each person choose 1 finger. Take turns rolling fingers on the pad and then on the paper.

3. Let the fingerprints dry.

4. Display the pages with each person's fingerprints on them.

5. Put the small pieces of paper with the fingerprints in a pile. Have each person take one.

6. See who is first to match the fingerprint to a person.

Showing What You Know

Use a large piece of poster board to make a set of class fingerprints. Put each person's name under his or her prints. Play the mystery-print game again. Use the class poster to identify mystery prints from people in the class.

Activity **6**

The Moon Above You

Why does the shape of the moon change? Find out. Then figure out why the moon looks the way it does tonight.

WORDS YOU NEED

revolve—to move around another body, such as a planet or a moon

gravity—a strong pull that all planets and stars have

phases—the different shapes the moon appears to have

crescent moon—the phase when you can see less than half of the moon

gibbous moon—the phase when you can see more than half of the moon

MAKE A PLAN

Here is what you will need.

_____ a clipboard   _____ a pencil

Review the activity. Estimate how long it will take.

_____

I will work

_____ by myself   _____ with a partner   _____ in a group

Did You Know . . .

It's hot during the day on the moon. When the sun is overhead, the temperature is 117 degrees Celsius (243 degrees Fahrenheit). That's hotter than boiling water!

At night, the temperature drops. The temperature at night may be minus 163 degrees Celsius (minus 261 degrees Fahrenheit).

A sunny day on the moon could kill you. But then, so could the night. That is one reason astronauts wore spacesuits on the moon.

Doing Research

The moon **revolves**, or travels, around Earth. The moon does this because **gravity** pulls it. Gravity is the pulling action of large objects such as planets and stars.

Most nights, the moon is the brightest thing in the sky. This is because it reflects light from the sun.

What we see of the moon changes from night to night. The shapes the moon appears to have are the **phases** of the moon.

- When we cannot see the moon at all, the moon is between the sun and Earth. This is called a new moon.

- When the moon is full, the moon is behind Earth and the sun shines on it.

The drawing below shows the different phases of the moon.

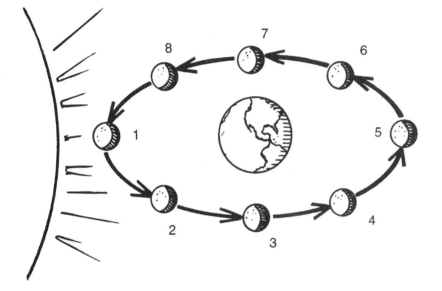

1. **New Moon**—You can't see the moon even though no clouds cover it.

2 & 8. **Crescent Moon**—You can see less than half of the moon.

3 & 7. **Half Moon**—You can see half of the moon.

4 & 6. **Gibbous Moon**—You can see more than half of the moon.

5. **Full Moon**—You can see the whole moon.

The drawings below show the phases of the moon as you see them from Earth.

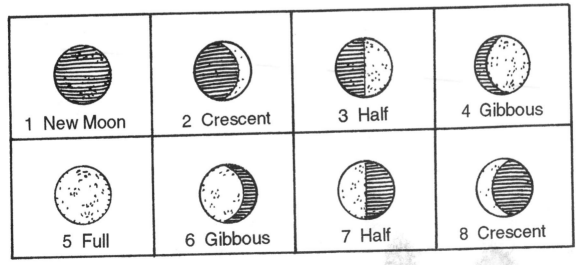

| 1 New Moon | 2 Crescent | 3 Half | 4 Gibbous |
| 5 Full | 6 Gibbous | 7 Half | 8 Crescent |

Collecting Information

Tonight, the moon will be in the sky. It may be full. It may be a tiny sliver. You may not be able to see it at all.

☑ Go outside tonight. Draw the shape of the moon in the first box below. If it is a cloudy night, don't do anything. Wait for a clear night.

☑ Check the shape of the moon four days later. Draw it in the second box.

☑ Check the shape of the moon in another four days. Draw it in the third box.

Date: _____ **Date:** _____ **Date:** _____

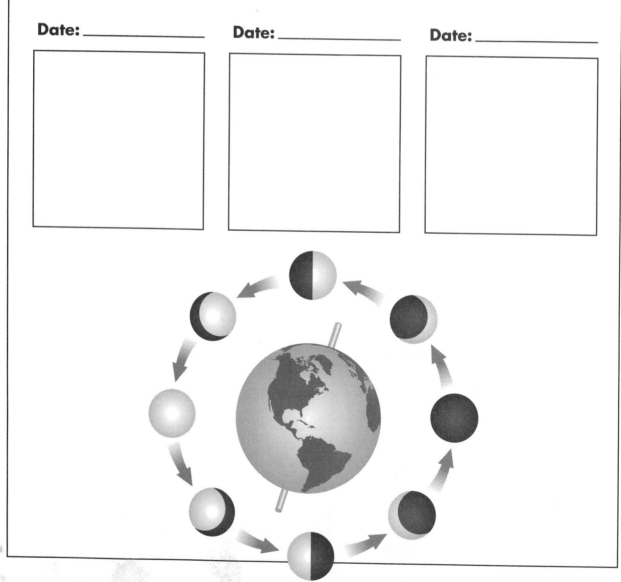

Analyzing Information

1. What phase was the moon in when you did the first drawing? _____

2. What phase was the moon in when you did the second drawing? _____

3. What phase was the moon in when you did the third drawing? _____

4. What will the phase of the moon be next?

_____

Showing What You Know

Plan a talk about the phases of the moon. Make sure these things are in your presentation.

☑ A model or a diagram that shows the phases of the moon.

☑ A description of why the phases of the moon change.

When your talk is ready, give it to a classmate first. Then ask your classmate these questions. The answers will show if he or she understands what you presented.

☑ Why does the moon shine at night?

☑ What is a phase of the moon?

☑ Why do the phases of the moon change?

Activity **7**

What Is That Landform?

*Earth is made up of **landforms**. Landforms are features of Earth's surface. In this activity, learn to identify landforms. Then label them.*

WORDS YOU NEED

landform—a feature of Earth's surface

mountain—a tall, steep landmass

plain—a low, flat landmass

plateau—a high, flat landmass

elevation—how high something is

MAKE A PLAN

Here is what you will need.

_____ 3 pieces of poster board   _____ markers

_____ old magazines and newspapers   _____ glue

_____ scissors

Review the activity. Estimate how long it will take.

_____

I will work

_____ by myself   _____ with a partner   _____ in a group

Did You Know . . .

For mountain climbers, Mount Everest is the top. It is the world's tallest mountain, at 8,850 meters (29,029 feet). The first person to reach the top was Sir Percival Hillary. He climbed Mount Everest in 1953.

Doing Research

There are three main kinds of landforms. They are
mountains, **plains**, and **plateaus** (plah-TOHZ). You can tell
a landform by its **elevation** and its shape. Its elevation is how
high a landform is. Its shape tells if it is flat, hilly, or peaked.

A mountain is a landform that reaches a high elevation. A
mountain is at least 600 meters (1,970 feet) above the land
around it.

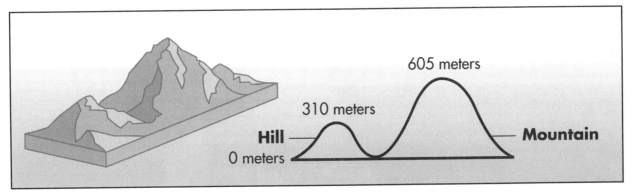

A plain is a large, flat area of land. It does not have a high
elevation.

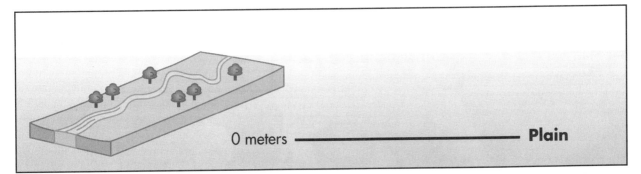

A plateau is a large, flat area of land. It is at a higher
elevation than a plain.

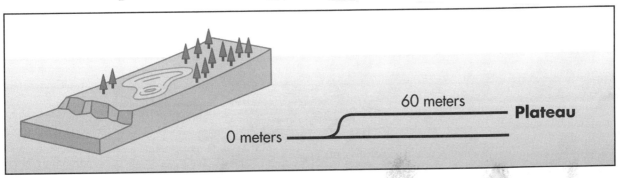

Collecting Information

Think about the land where you live. Here is a map of the United States. Many major landforms are shown on the map.

▲ Mountains

ᴗᴗ Plains

◺ Plateaus

Find where you live on the map.

What is the main landform where you live?

_____

Look through old magazines. Locate pictures of landforms. Carefully cut them out. Look in books for pictures of landforms. Make copies of the pictures. You may also draw them.

Analyzing Information

1. Sort the pictures. Place the pictures of mountains in one pile. Place the pictures of plains in another. Place the pictures of plateaus in a third pile.

2. Get a piece of poster board. Write "Mountains" at the top with a marker. Glue the pictures of mountains to the poster board.

3. Label a second piece of poster board "Plains." Glue the pictures of plains to the poster board.

4. Label a third piece of the poster board "Plateaus." Glue the pictures of plateaus to the poster board.

Showing What You Know

Use your posters to make a display of the landforms. Make a label for each poster. On the labels, write about the landform. What is a landform? How can you identify a landform?

Activity 8

What Is the Weather?

The weather changes every day. Reading a weather map can help you in everyday life. Find out how to read a weather map. Then use the map to plan a trip.

WORDS YOU NEED

front—the place where cold and hot air meet

high pressure—an area where air pressure is low. High pressure often brings good weather.

low pressure—an area where air pressure is high. Low pressure often brings storms.

MAKE A PLAN

Here is what you will need.

_____ pencil   _____ road map of the United States

_____ marker   _____ weather map from a newspaper

Review the activity. Estimate how long it will take.

_____

I will work

_____ by myself _____ with a partner _____ in a group

Did You Know . . .

The hottest temperature in the United States was recorded at Death Valley, California. It was 57 degrees Celsius (134 degrees Fahrenheit).

The coldest temperature in the United States was minus 62 degrees Celsius (minus 79 degrees Fahrenheit), in Prospect Creek, Alaska.

Louisiana is the wettest state in the United States. It receives 142 centimeters (56 inches) of rain each year.

The driest state is Nevada. Only 23 centimeters (9 inches) of rain falls there each year.

When you know what the weather will be, you can dress comfortably. You can also plan your activities.

Doing Research

Look at the weather map. The key tells what the symbols on the map mean.

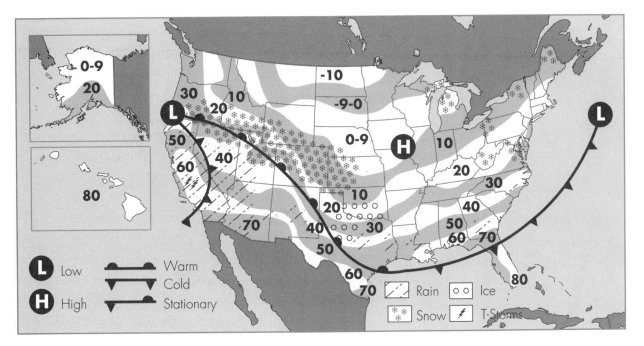

A **front** is the place where cold air and hot air meet. On a weather map, the line showing a front looks like this:

There are different kinds of fronts.

- A cold front is an edge of cold air. It forms when cold air moves against warm air. A cold front causes warm air to become cold. Often, rain or snow forms near a cold front.

- A warm front is an edge of warm air. When warm air meets cold air, the warm front moves above the cool air. Rain or snow often falls. Then the air becomes warm.

Look for this symbol on the map: H.

- It means **high pressure**. High pressure brings clear weather. Winds blow out of high-pressure areas.

Look for this symbol on the map: L.

- This symbol means **low pressure**. If you see this symbol, watch out. Low pressure often means bad weather. Winds rush into a low-pressure area. These winds bring storms.

Collecting Information

Look at this weather map.

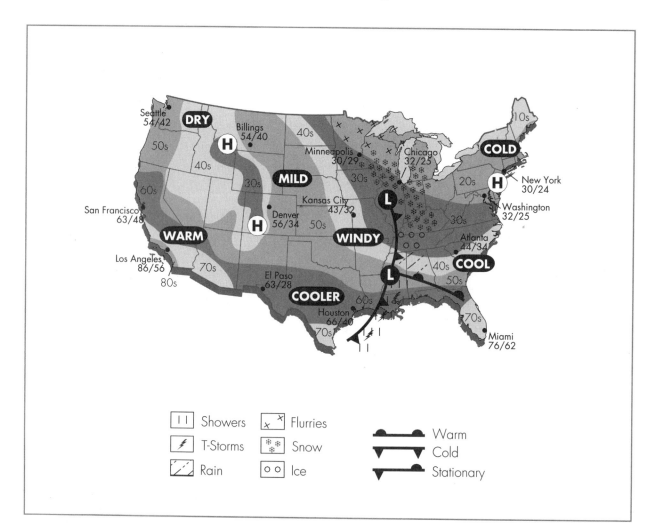

The key on the map shows what the symbols mean.

1. Where is it raining? How do you know? _____

_____

2. Where is it snowing? How do you know? _____

_____

3. Where is there likely to be a storm? Why? _____

_____

4. Where is the weather clear? How do you know? _____

_____

Analyzing Information

Get a map that shows major roads of the United States. Also find the weather map in a newspaper.

Plan a trip across the country for a friend. Your friend will go from San Francisco to Washington, D.C.

As you plan the trip, keep these tips in mind:

☑ Try not to go where there is bad weather. Go around it.

☑ Use main highways for the trip. They are quicker.

☑ Trace the trip on the map first. Use a marker to do this.

☑ Write out the route on a sheet of paper.

☑ Write the cities and states through which the route passes.

☑ Tell your friend what kind of weather to expect during the trip.

Showing What You Know

Show your route to a friend.

☑ Give your friend written instructions that describe your route.

☑ Show your friend the route on the map.

☑ Show your friend where to expect bad weather. Tell him or her what kind of weather it will be.

☑ Ask your friend if he or she understands the route and the weather to expect.

Activity 9

Hard Rocks

You can classify rocks by how hard they are. Find out how to do this. Then classify some rocks.

MAKE A PLAN

Here is what you will need.

_____ at least 5 different kinds of rocks   _____ penny

_____ small piece of safety glass   _____ steel nail

_____ small pieces of paper   _____ tape

Review the activity. Estimate how long it will take.

_____

I will work

_____ by myself   _____ with a partner   _____ in a group

WORDS YOU NEED

minerals—natural solids formed from earth materials

classify—to arrange in groups

Did You Know . . .

The hardest material in the world is the same as one of the softest. Look at a pencil. The part of the pencil you write with is made of graphite. Graphite is made of carbon.

What do you think the hardest material in the world is? Circle your guess.

Steel

Diamond

Copper

Gold

The answer? A diamond. Like graphite, it is made of carbon.

Doing Research

All rocks are made of **minerals**. A mineral is formed from the materials in the earth. Gold is a mineral. A diamond is also a mineral.

Scientists can **classify** rocks. When you classify rocks, you group them.

There are many ways to classify rocks. You can classify rocks by color. You can classify rocks by how they feel. You can also classify rocks by how hard they are.
How do you think knowing the hardness of a rock might be useful? _____

• A German named Friedrich Mohs found a way to test minerals for hardness. It is called the Mohs scale.

• His test is based on scratching minerals. A hard mineral will scratch a softer one. A soft mineral will not scratch a harder one. Minerals are listed based on how hard they are to scratch.

• On the Mohs scale, a diamond is the hardest mineral. Talc, which is often a powder, is the softest.

Mohs Scale of Hardness

Mineral	Hardness	Mineral	Hardness
Talc	1	Feldspar	6
Gypsum	2	Quartz	7
Calcite	3	Topaz	8
Fluorite	4	Corundum	9
Apatite	5	Diamond	10

Knowing how hard a mineral is could come in handy. Imagine that you were drilling through steel. Steel has a hardness of 6 on the Mohs scale. You would want a drill that is harder than that. You could use a diamond drill. Then you would be sure that the drill would work.

Collecting Information

1. Collect at least five rocks that look and feel different from one another.

2. Place the rocks on a desk.

3. Write the numbers 1 to 5 on small pieces of paper. Place a numbered paper under each rock. Use the number labels to tell which rock is which.

4. Test the rocks. **Be careful!** The nail and the glass could cut you. To test each rock, do this.

☑ Try to scratch the rock with your fingernail.

☑ Try to scratch the rock with a penny.

☑ Try to scratch the rock with the steel nail.

☑ Hold the safety glass firmly on the desk. Carefully rub a rock over the surface of the glass. Look to see if the rock scratched the glass.

☑ Find out where the rock fits on the Mohs scale below. Write the number of the rock in the correct place.

☑ Repeat steps 1–5 for the rest of the rocks.

Field Test for Rock Hardness

Hardness	Rock Number	Test
1 2		Fingernail will scratch it.
3		Fingernail will not scratch it. Penny will.
4 5		Penny will not scratch it. Steel nail or glass will.
6 7 8 9		Will scratch a steel nail. Will scratch glass.
10		Will scratch anything but diamonds.

Analyzing Information

Place all of the rocks on your desk. Use the Mohs scale to classify the rocks in order from the softest to the hardest.

Use your rocks to check your results. Remember that a rock will scratch only those rocks softer than it. The softest rock should not be able to scratch any other rock. The hardest rock should scratch every other rock.

Showing What You Know

Give a demonstration for your class.

☑ On the chalkboard, draw a Mohs scale like the one on page 36. Tell the class about the Mohs hardness scale.

☑ Show them the rocks that you tested. Explain the tests that you used.

☑ Let your classmates take turns testing the rocks. Write the results on your Mohs scale.

☑ See if the class gets the same results that you did.

☑ Ask the class why knowing a rock's hardness is important. After they guess, tell them how a diamond drill could be useful in cutting other hard rocks.

Field Test for Rock Hardness

Hardness	Rock Number	Test
1 2		Fingernail will scratch it.
3		Fingernail will not scratch it. Penny will.
4 5		Penny will not scratch it. Steel nail or glass will.
6 7 8 9		Will scratch a steel nail. Will scratch glass.
10		Will scratch anything but diamonds.

Activity 10
How Your Town Recycles

You will find out how people recycle in your town. Then you will make a poster to help people learn how to recycle.

MAKE A PLAN

Here is what you will need.

_____ pencil   _____ telephone

_____ poster board   _____ paint or markers

Review the activity. Estimate how long it will take.

_____

I will work

_____ by myself   _____with a partner   _____in a group

Did You Know . . .

What do you think takes up the most space in dumps? Circle your guess.

WORDS YOU NEED

resource—a material that can be used for another purpose

nonrenewable—not able to be replaced

recycle—to change something so it can be used for something else

reuse—to use something again

reduce—to use less of something

Doing Research

Why do we need to throw less away? There are two reasons. One is that some **resources** are **nonrenewable**. That means there is only a certain amount of that resource in the world. One example of this is oil. When we use up all the oil in the world, there will be no more.

There is another reason to throw less away. All of our trash has to be put somewhere. Often, it is put into garbage dumps. Much of that trash will be there for hundreds of years. The dumps fill up with all this trash.

There are three ways we can cut down on trash.

One way is to **recycle**. When you recycle something, it is made into another shape and used again. Old newspapers may become paper bags. A glass jar can be melted and made into a bottle.

Another way to cut down on trash is to **reuse** things. You can wash and use again a bottle that held mustard.

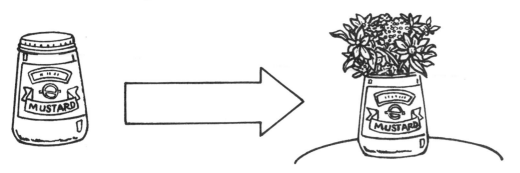

The third way to cut down on trash is to **reduce** the amount of trash you make. Stop buying things that you don't need in the first place. That reduces the amount of the earth's resources that you use.

Collecting Information

Does your town have rules for recycling? You can find out.

1. Find the phone number for the mayor's office. Write it here. _____

2. Call the mayor's office. Ask to speak to the person who knows about recycling. Then ask these questions.

What can be recycled? Circle the right things.

Newspapers

Other Paper

Cans

Plastic

Glass

Motor Oil

3. Where should people take things to be recycled?

_____

_____

_____

4. When should people recycle?

_____

_____

5. What happens to the things that people recycle?

_____

_____

Analyzing Information

Use what you have learned to make a poster to help people in your town. Look at the notes you took.

What do people need to know if they want to recycle? How could you show that on a poster?

Make sure your poster shows these things.

- ☑ What can be recycled
- ☑ Where things are recycled
- ☑ When things should be recycled
- ☑ Why recycling is important

Here are some examples of posters that you could make.

Showing What You Know

When you have finished your poster, answer these questions.

1. Who would want to see this poster? _____

_____

2. Where could you put this poster so those people would see it? _____

_____

Plan where to hang your poster. Ask if you can put it there. Then, if you have permission, hang it up to show others how to recycle.

Activity 11

What Is the Change?

Some changes are physical. Some are chemical. Do you know the difference? Find out. Cause some physical and chemical changes in matter. Then show your family what you learned.

MAKE A PLAN

Here is what you will need.

_____ 1/2 cup milk   _____ 3 clear plastic cups

_____ ice cubes   _____ spoon

_____ vinegar   _____ baking soda

_____ plastic wrap   _____ rubber band

Review the activity. Estimate how long it will take.

_____

I will work

_____ by myself   _____with a partner   _____ in a group

Did You Know . . .

Your eyes may water when you peel an onion. Your eyes
water because of a chemical change.

What causes your eyes to water? A gas is given off by the
cut onion. It goes to your eyes. The gas meets the salty
water in your eyes. A chemical change takes place. The salt
and the gas form an acid. The acid causes your eyes to sting.

Doing Research

Two kinds of changes affect matter. One is a **physical change**. The other is a **chemical change**.

Here's how to tell the difference.

A *physical change* changes the way that something looks. It does not change what something is made of. When you crumple a piece of paper, it is still a piece of paper. Only the size and shape of the paper are changed. Crumpling is a physical change.

When you boil water, some of the water goes into the air. It changes to steam. Steam forms when water changes from a liquid to a gas. Steam does not look the same as water, but it is still water. Changing water to steam is a *physical change*.

A *chemical change* changes matter to make a new material. If you burn a sheet of paper, the paper changes. The paper turns to ashes. Ashes are not the same as paper. They are made from different materials. Burning paper to form ashes is a chemical change.

Here is another chemical change. What happens if you leave your bicycle out in the rain? It rusts. The rust is not the same as the metal in your bicycle. Rust is a new material. Because a new material forms, rusting is a *chemical change*.

Collecting Information

You will make some changes in matter. Then you will decide whether they are physical or chemical changes.

To do this, follow these steps. **Wear your safety goggles and laboratory apron during this activity.**

1. Pour some milk into a cup. Look at and smell the milk. Do not taste the milk. Describe its color and smell.

_____

2. Cover the cup with plastic wrap. Hold the wrap in place with a rubber band. Put it aside for 2 days. Then look at it and smell it. Do not taste the milk. Describe any changes you observe.

_____

_____

3. Put two ice cubes into another cup. Look at the ice cubes. Describe their shape and color.

_____

_____

4. Put the cup with the ice on your desk for a half-hour. Then look at it. Describe what you see.

_____

_____

5. Put one spoonful of baking soda into a cup. Look at it. Describe its color and texture.

_____

6. Add one spoonful of vinegar to the cup with the baking soda. Describe the changes that you see.

_____

_____

Analyzing Information

Look at your notes on the last page. Think about what a physical change is. Think about what a chemical change is. Use your notes to answer these questions.

1. Which changes were physical? _____

_____

2. Why were they physical changes? _____

_____

3. Which changes were chemical? _____

_____

4. Why were they chemical changes? _____

_____

Showing What You Know

Demonstrate to your family what you learned.

☑ At home, set up the same activity that you did on page 44.

☑ Tell your family what you will be doing.

☑ Wait until all the materials have changed.

☑ Explain which changes are physical. Explain which changes are chemical.

Activity 12

Is Your Water Acidic?

You may think that all water is the same. It isn't. Some water is more acidic or more basic than other water. Test different kinds of water. Then make a chart to show what you found out.

WORDS YOU NEED

acid rain—rain that has mixed with air pollution and becomes acid. It is harmful to plants and animals.

neutral—a substance that is neither an acid or a base

acid—a substance that reacts with metals and forms hydrogen. Acids are sour.

base—a substance that is formed when a metal reacts with water. Bases are bitter.

MAKE A PLAN

Here is what you will need.

_____ 3 plastic cups   _____ lab coat
_____ goggles   _____ red and blue litmus paper
_____ labels   _____ baking soda
_____ vinegar   _____ pond or river water
_____ rain or snow   _____ puddle water
_____ tap water

Review the activity. Estimate how long it will take.

_____

I will work

_____ by myself   _____ with a partner   _____ in a group

Did You Know . . .

Trees in some of the world's largest forests are dying. Fish in lakes and streams are dying. Why?

The problem is **acid rain**. Acid rain is caused by air pollution. It falls on trees and fish. Sometimes, it kills them.

Doing Research

Pure water is **neutral**. A substance that is neutral is not an acid or a base. Vinegar is an **acid**. Baking soda is a **base**.

You can use litmus paper to find out whether a substance is an acid or a base. There are two kinds of litmus paper: red and blue. Here is how they work.

In acid: red litmus paper stays red.
                blue litmus paper turns red.

In a base: red litmus paper turns blue.
                blue litmus paper stays blue.

If it is neutral: red litmus paper stays red.
                blue litmus paper stays blue.

You can test how each kind of litmus paper acts. First, put on your safety goggles and a laboratory apron.

1. Pour some vinegar into a plastic cup. Touch a piece of red litmus paper to the vinegar. What happens to the color of the litmus paper?

_____

2. Touch a piece of blue litmus paper to the vinegar. What happens to the color of the litmus paper?

_____

3. Put a spoonful of baking soda into a cup. Fill the cup halfway with distilled water. Stir the mixture. Touch a piece of red litmus paper to the mixture. What happens to the color of the litmus paper?

_____

4. Touch a piece of blue litmus paper to the water. What happens to the color of the litmus paper?

_____

Collecting Information

You will use red and blue litmus paper to find out whether water samples are acids or bases.

1. Put each sample into a clean plastic cup. Make a label for each cup. On each label, write where the water came from. Put the labels on the cups.

2. Put on your laboratory coat and goggles. Test each sample with the red litmus paper. Write the color of the paper on the chart for each sample.

3. Test each sample with the blue litmus paper. Write the color of the paper for each sample on the chart.

What is the sample?	When was it taken?	Colors in red litmus paper	Colors in blue litmus paper

Analyzing Information

Look at your chart. Use the chart to answer these questions.

1. Which of your samples were basic? _____

How do you know? _____

2. Which of your samples were acidic? _____

How do you know? _____

3. Which of your samples were neutral? _____

How do you know? _____

Showing What You Know

Combine the information in your chart with the information of your classmates. Make a class chart. It should look like this.

What is the sample?	When was it taken?	Colors in red litmus paper	Colors in blue litmus paper	Your initials
tap water	3/8	red	red	N.W.

☑ Then have each person write the information he or she found on the chart. Each person should put his or her initials next to the information.

☑ Talk about what your class found out. Is most of the water you tested acid or base? How could a scientist use this information to help the environment?

Activity 13

Machines Are Simple

*A **machine** makes work easier. All machines are made with some basic parts. Find some machines at your house. Then explain how they make your life easier.*

WORDS YOU NEED

machine—a device that makes work easier

simple machine—a machine that does work with only one movement

inclined plane—a slanted surface used to raise an object

wedge—an inclined plane that moves

screw—an inclined plane that is wrapped around a post to form a spiral

lever—a bar that moves around a fixed point

wheel and axle—a lever that moves in a circle

pulley—a chain or rope that is wrapped around a wheel

complex machine—a machine that is made up of two or more simple machines

MAKE A PLAN

Here is what you will need.

_____ a pencil _____ a clipboard with paper

Review the activity. Estimate how long it will take.

_____

I will work

_____ by myself _____ with a partner _____ in a group

Did You Know . . .

What would the world be like without machines? There would be

no cars   no shovels

Doing Research

There are six kinds of **simple machines**. Simple machines do work with only one movement. They are:

The **inclined plane**. An inclined plane is a slanted surface that is used to raise something. It connects a low place to a high place. It is easier to move something up an inclined plane than to lift it.

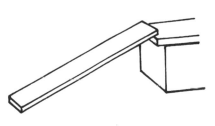

The **wedge**. A wedge is an inclined plane that moves. Most wedges are really two inclined planes put together. A wedge can push things apart.

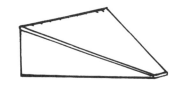

The **screw**. A screw is an inclined plane that is wrapped around a post to form a spiral.

The **lever**. A lever is a bar that moves around a fixed point. Look at this picture. It shows how a lever can help you move something more easily.

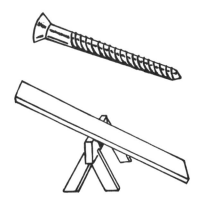

The **wheel and axle**. A wheel and axle is a lever that moves in a circle. The larger circle (the wheel) moves the smaller circle (the axle).

The **pulley**. A pulley is a chain or rope that is wrapped around a wheel. A pulley can help you lift heavy things.

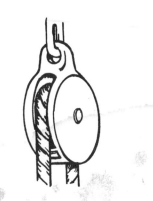

Collecting Information

For one day, look for examples of simple machines. (Remember that a **complex machine** is made up of two or more simple machines.) Take notes when you see a simple machine. Carry your clipboard with you. When you see a machine, do the following.

1. Draw a picture of the machine that you see.

2. Write where you saw it.

3. Write what it does.

4. Write what kind of simple machine it is.

Here is what one of your pages might look like:

See-Saw in Park – Lever

Helps Kids move Up and Down

Analyzing Information

Look at your notes about the machines that you saw.

1. Circle the simple machines that you saw.

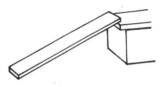

inclined plane

lever

wheel and axle

wedge

pulley

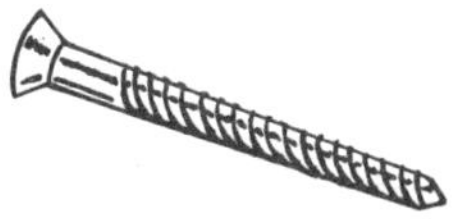

screw

2. Choose one machine that you saw. Describe how it makes work easier.

_____

_____

_____

Showing What You Know

Think about the machine that you just wrote about. Write how your life would be different without that machine.

_____

_____

_____

_____

_____

Activity 14

Wrap It Up

What's the best way to keep a cup of hot water hot? Test some different ways. Then design a cup holder to keep water hot.

MAKE A PLAN

Here is what you will need.

_____ 4 paper cups that can hold hot water

_____ thick cotton cloth _____ candy thermometer

_____ plastic bags _____ newspaper

_____ tape _____ hot water

Review the activity. Estimate how long it will take.

_____

I will work

_____ by myself _____ with a partner _____ in a group

WORDS YOU NEED

insulation—materials that keep in heat

insulators—materials that do not allow heat to move through them easily

conductors—materials that let heat move through them easily

Did You Know . . .

The sea otter lives in very cold oceans. It is also the only ocean mammal that has a thick layer of fat. In other animals, that fat keeps them warm.

How can the otter live in such cold water? The secret is in its fur. A sea otter cleans its fur many times each day. This keeps a layer of air inside the fur. That air keeps the otter warm.

Doing Research

Have you ever been outside on a cold day without a coat?

Soon, you became cold. You became cold because you lost the heat of your body to the air around you. Unlike the otter, you had no **insulation** against the cold.

- Some materials are **insulators**. Heat does not travel easily through them.

Think of when you put on a heavy wool coat to go outside. Wool is an insulator. Heat does not move through it easily. The wool insulates you. It keeps the heat from your body from going into the air.

- Some materials are **conductors** of heat. Conductors let heat travel through them easily.

What happens when you heat water on a stove? You place the water in a metal pan. The heat from the stove travels through the pan quickly and heats the water in the pan. The metal conducts the heat.

Collecting Information

Find out which material works best to keep the water in a cup hot. Here's what you will do.

1. Wrap plastic bags around a cup. Tape the bags in place.

2. Wrap several layers of newspaper around another cup. Tape the newspaper in place.

3. Wrap several layers of the cotton cloth around a third cup. Tape the cloth in place.

4. Leave one cup alone. This cup will show what happens if you do nothing.

5. Pour a half cup of hot water into each cup. Use the thermometer to measure the temperature of the water in each cup. Write the temperature on the chart on this page.

6. After 30 minutes, take the temperature of the water in each cup again. Shake the thermometer between tests for an accurate reading. Write the temperature of the water in each cup on the chart.

What's in the cup?	Starting temperature of water	Temperature of water after 30 minutes	Amount of change

Analyzing Information

Look at the chart. Use the chart to answer the questions.

1. Which material was the best insulator? Explain your answer.

_____

2. Which material was the best conductor? Explain your answer.

_____

3. What material would you choose to keep a cup warm?

_____

Showing What You Know

Design a cup holder to keep water hot.

1. Choose the material that you think will keep the water in the cup hot.

2. How could you make a cup holder of that material? Draw some ideas here.

3. Make the cup holder.

4. Create a class display of cup insulators.

Activity 15

What Is Color?

What color is light? Find out in this activity. Then make a spinner to prove what you found out.

MAKE A PLAN

Here is what you will need.

_____ scissors   _____ white, thin cardboard

_____ straight pin   _____ pencil with eraser

_____ red, blue, and green markers or paint

Review the activity. Estimate how long it will take.

_____

I will work

_____ by myself   _____with a partner   _____ in a group

WORDS YOU NEED

visible spectrum—the seven colors that make up white light

absorbed—taken into an object

reflected—bounced off an object

Did You Know . . .

A rainbow forms when light passes through drops of water. The drops separate the white light of the sun into colors.

The longest a rainbow has ever lasted is 3 hours. This rainbow formed in Great Britain in 1979.

Doing Research

White light is made up of seven colors. These colors form the **visible spectrum**. When the seven colors of the visible spectrum combine, they form white light.

How do we see colors? Like this.

Imagine that you are looking at a red wall. The wall **absorbed** all the colors of light in the visible spectrum except for red light. The red light is **reflected** from the wall. This is the color you see.

- Objects that absorb all colors of light look black.
- Objects that reflect all colors of light look white.

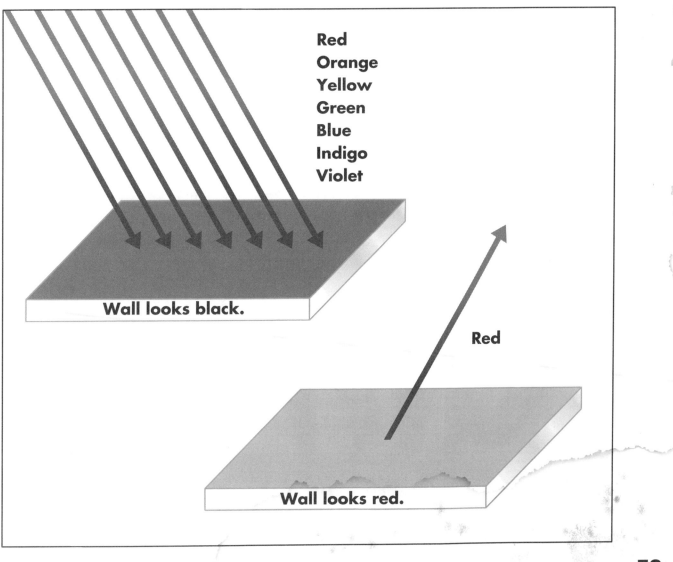

Red
Orange
Yellow
Green
Blue
Indigo
Violet

Wall looks black.

Red

Wall looks red.

Collecting Information

You can prove that white light is made up of all the colors of light. To do this, make a spinner.

1. Trace the circle on this page onto a thin piece of white cardboard.

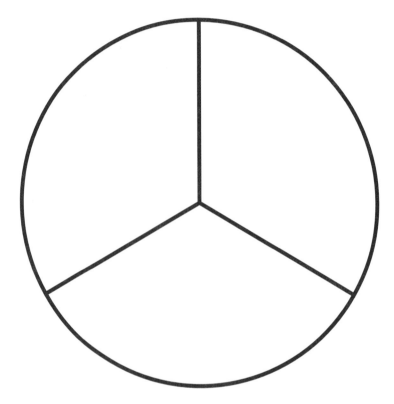

2. On your circle, lightly draw in 3 lines.

3. Color one section of the circle blue.

4. Color one section of the circle red.

5. Color one section of the circle green.

6. Carefully use scissors to cut out your circle.

7. Carefully stick the pin through the center of the circle. Then push the pin into the eraser of a pencil.

8. Spin the color wheel as quickly as you can. Observe the color of the wheel as it spins. Record your observations.

_____

_____

Analyzing Information

1. Describe what you saw when you spun the wheel quickly.

_____

2. Why do you think that you saw this?

_____

_____

Showing What You Know

Show your class what you learned.

1. Ask what will happen if you spin the color wheel.

2. Let a student spin the color wheel quickly.

3. Explain why the color appears white. (It may seem gray-white or muddy if the colors are not clear.)